THE ADVENTURES OF

Cammy
LAMBIE

IN THE PLACE OF THE BIG BLUE SKY

Written & Illustrated by
Mara-lee Stricker

This book is dedicated to Little Lambie
Ezra Soterio Perez (Isaiah 62:1)
We will see you in heaven, precious one
Love, Grammy

SPECIAL THANKS

To The Great Shepherd who has given His life for
His sheep.

To my husband, Greg, for his love and encouragement.

Thank you to my mother, Donna Lapp, who graciously
walked through each page for hours with me over the phone
to help with editing.

A huge thanks to my pastor and earthly shepherd, Jeff
Durbin, who has given his careful attention to making sure
that this book stayed faithful to the words of our Great
Shepherd.

To my church, Apologia, where I was introduced to the
catechism truths of God's word, and
www.desiringgod.com.

To my prayer team who helped me pray this book through!

To Tim Schweitzer and Nikki Watson for helping me
reformat and remaster this book.

CHAPTER 1

WHO IS GOD?

S pring had come to the grazing meadows and the little lambs were bounding amidst the growing flock. The Shepherd[1] was busy tending to his barn as he readied for new life daily.

Every morning Cammy lambie cuddled close to his mother until the barn door was opened; then he would stand and stretch very big, and walk to the edge of his little pen, watching as several lambs and ewes rushed out into The Place of the Big Blue Sky.

Cammy lambie loved being near Mother. He and his brother, Sammy, would often play King of the Hill on Mother's back.

One night when the barn was quiet, Mother said, "Tomorrow is a special day."

"Why, Mother?" bleated Cammy.

Sammy peeked awake with one eye.

"I heard Shepherd say that you and Sammy could go out to The Place of the Big Blue Sky." Both lambs were wide awake now!

Grammy lambie was listening and she turned and laid her chin on the rung between their pens. "We have so much to teach you two."

Mother let out a little bleat² in agreement and smiled at her little rams. "God has made so much for us to enjoy."

"God?" questioned Cammy.

"Who is God?"
asked Sammy.

"Oh, that is a great question! God is the first and best of all beings!"
answered Mother.

"That's right," said Grammy. "He tells us that He is the first and the last, and that besides Him there is no god" (Isaiah 44:6).

"First ever?" inquired[3] Cammy.

"And last ever?" continued Sammy.

"Yes, and besides Him there is no other," Mother ewe nodded.

The little rams lay back down and snuggled close to her. They were happy that Mother and Grammy knew so much about God. It made them feel safe.

"Good night, young ones. Sleep well," Mother said, as she touched each of her lambs with her nose.

---

1. SHEPHERD: *a person who tends, feeds and guards herds*

2. BLEAT: *the sound a sheep or goat make*

3. INQUIRED: *to have sought information by questioning; asked*

CHAPTER 2

IN HIS PRESENCE

After morning feeding in the barn, Shepherd rolled back the big barn door. The place of the Big Blue Sky seemed especially bright, and Cammy squinted as the light grew stronger. Cammy and Sammy began to leap and bounce into each other, giggling and bleating. Today was a special day! They could hardly contain themselves!

"Please be sure to stay near me," Mother bleated cautiously. "Even though you are excited and want to run and jump, you must choose to follow Grammy lambie and me as we follow Shepherd."

"Shepherd has prepared a new pasture, I hear," Grammy said to Mother ewe. "He is going to lead us there, but we all need to follow Him."

"Yes," said Mother. "We all need to follow him. Cammy, will you follow Shepherd?" Cammy nodded. "Sammy, will you follow Shepherd?"

"Yes, Mother. I will," he replied.

Shepherd's helpers walked nearer and nearer, checking all of the sheep and their pens. Shepherd had told them which lambs were ready and which ones to pass by. Shepherd knew everything!

Soon it was their turn. Helper clicked their pen gate and swung it open. Mother ewe and the boys scurried out. Grammy followed close behind and everyone headed toward The Place of the Big Blue Sky.

Shepherd led the way, calling out to his beloved
sheep as he walked. "Here to me, sheep!"

"Baa!" Everyone bleated back with great
enthusiam[1].

"Here! Here to me!"

"Baa!"

Cammy and Sammy thrilled at all of the
commotion[2]. The Place of the Big Blue Sky opened
wider than they could've ever imagined. Everyone
was pushing and shoving as they followed at a quick
pace. Mother was still near her ram lambs, as was
Grammy.

"Mother, where are we going, and what will we do when we get there?" asked Cammy as he struggled to keep up.

Mother responded thoughtfully, "We are going to a new pasture. It is there that you and all the other new lambs will get to taste the sweet grass God has provided for us to enjoy."

Grammy confirmed. "Isn't that exciting, Cammy? God has provided things for us to enjoy! Shepherd will always lead us to a place to graze³ and rest because he is the best! Remember we told you last night that God is the first and best of all beings?"

The listening lambs nodded as she continued. "Because he is the best, he knows what we need. We can enjoy his provision. We can trust him. God tells us 'He will make known to us the path of life and in His presence is fullness of joy and in His right hand there are pleasures forevermore'" (Psalms 16:11)

"Wow," Cammy exclaimed! "I'm thankful for God! I'm thankful for Shepherd!" Immediately, he sprang into the air!

Grammy smiled at Mother ewe

"In His presence there is fullness of joy!"

Mother smiled and continued,

"... and in His right hand there are pleasures forevermore!"

"Are we there yet? I'm hungry" Sammy interrupted.
All he could think about was eating.

Just then, Shepherd called out "Here to me,
sheep!" and he stopped at a stone wall where a gate
stood open. The flock rushed in, Shepherd's staff
touching each one as they passed through the gate
to the new pasture.

Crunch! Munch! Crunch! Munch!

It was time to eat!

---

1. ENTHUSIAM: *strong excitement of feeling*

2. COMMOTION: *a noisy disturbance; violent motion*

3. GRAZE: *to feed on growing grass in a pasture*

CHAPTER 3

GOD REVEALS

Cammy couldn't decide if it was more fun to run and jump, or to munch on the sweet grass.

Was the grass sweeter here on this side of Mother, or on that side nearer to Grammy?

The Place of the Big Blue Sky seemed to grow as Cammy chewed grass and looked out at the rest of the flock.

"Baa!" Each mother sheep called out to her lambs from time to time, and the lambs would respond in kind. This was the way that they kept tabs on each other by listening for each other's voices.

Each little family group stayed together.

Cammy put his head down to eat some more. He found a little patch of clover and followed it.

"Mmmm" he munched. "Mmmm."

He moved over a little more and kept munching.

"This is so good."

"Oh, my! What is that?" Cammy spotted something in the shadow of a big rock.

As he walked toward the shadow, he heard the voice
of his mother in his heart warning him "please be
sure to stay near me." He let out a little bleat to see
if Mother was close as he enjoyed the clover and
walked closer to the rock.

The shadow had two eyes. Cammy felt afraid. He
called out to his family.

"Baa!" Mother did not answer.

"Baa!" Sammy did not answer.

The little ram lamb quickly turned, bleated loudly, and ran back to where he could see his family. Mother called out too, as she ran towards Cammy. "Baa!" She scolded him in a firm tone. "Where were you, Cammy?"

"I was over by the shadow." Cammy felt very ashamed[1].

The two of them quickly trotted toward Grammy and the rest of the flock.

"Many shadows are not our friends," said Mother.

"Many shadows are not our friends," echoed Grammy.

"Don't you remember me telling you 'please be sure to stay near' before we left the barn this morning?" Cammy reflected² upon the voice of his mother. Then he heard it again, 'please be sure to stay near.'

"Yes, Mother. I heard your voice in my heart. I'm sorry. I'm sorry I walked away." He was very repentant.

"I know, Cammy, and I forgive you. I'm glad you are safe. I love you." She snuggled him and bleated softly. Her voice never sounded so sweet.

As they snuggled, Cammy thought about the voice he had heard in his heart. "Mother, how did I hear a voice in my heart?"

Mother smiled and answered wisely. "The voice in your heart is called 'your conscience³.' That voice can also be called 'the light of nature' because it illuminates what is right. (John 1:4)

This is the law of God written on your heart,
Cammy (Romans 2:15)! In fact, everyone was
created with this same revelation⁴. We all have the
truth of God written on our hearts. It is important
to heed His voice."

Times of careful discipline can also be the times of
sweetest teaching, and so Mother continued. "Boys,
God is so good to us. He teaches us about Himself
in so many ways. Besides our consciences, He also
teaches us about Himself through His works in
nature.

This is called 'general revelation.' He shows us
He is our provider by giving us clover as food. He
proves He is our rest by giving us peaceful meadow
to sleep in. He teaches us about His faithfulness
with the sun that rises and sets everyday! He is
faithful AND He is our light! Can you see how
clearly He declares Himself to us?" The boys
nodded.

Grammy jumped in. "There is one more way that He confirms Himself again to us… The Bible. This is also called 'special revelation.' Let me give you an example: In the Bible God tells us to obey our parents (Ephesians 6:1). God revealed this law to you through the voice of instruction you heard in your conscience. It is important for you to obey those who love you and watch out for you. It is important to obey God's word, the Bible."

"So, again," Mother repeated for clarity, "God reveals Himself to us in 'the light of nature,' which is our conscience. He reveals Himself through 'general revelation,' the nature around us. And then, lastly, He reveals Himself through 'special revelation,' the Bible."

Grammy finished by saying "Each of these three revelations confirms the other two ways. They never go against each other... never contradict. If we hear a voice in our head telling us something that does not agree with what God's word says is true, we are not listening to the right voice. If God wrote it, that is the real truth and we can trust it because God is trustworthy. He never lies. It's not in His nature to lie" (Numbers 23:19).

"His word says 'Since the creation of the world, His invisible attributes, His eternal power, and His divine nature have been clearly seen, being understood through what has been made by Him so that man is without excuse"

Romans 1:19-20

"What do you mean, 'without excuse?'" Cammy asked.

"It means that no one can say they can't see God because He has clearly shown Himself in His creation! No one can say they didn't know about God because He clearly tells us about Himself in His written word," answered Grammy. Cammy nodded as he looked around. He could see God was great by the greatness of the Big Blue Sky. He could see God is Love, because he could feel the love of Mother and Grammy.

Sammy wasn't as interested in all this talk. He found a little ant to watch, and soon found himself drifting off into dreamland. He dreamt of clouds and clover, snakes and snails, how big his horns would be when he grew up... and he dreamt of eating.

---

1. ASHAMED: *distressed of embarrassed by feelings of guilt, foolishness, or disgrace*
2. REFLECTED: *to think back upon a previous experience.*
3. CONSCIENCE: *the inner sense of what is right or wrong in one's conduct or motives, pushing one toward right action*
4. REVELATION: *a surprising and previously unknown fact that is made known*

CHAPTER 4

GOD IS SPIRIT

Several hours had passed. Several hours of napping, munching, leaping, and thinking about God.

Sammy and Cammy romped and rolled, always making sure to stay within range of their mother's call. All of a sudden, Cammy had a thought. He knew who to ask, so he ran over to Mother.

"God is good to help us in so many ways," Cammy decided. "But, I've been thinking," he said as he lifted his head to look at a passing cloud and catch his breath. "I was far away from you when I heard your voice in my heart. How did God know? I was not near you!"

"I think you are noticing something else very special about God, Cammy...

"He is spirit!"
Mother answered

"God is spirit[1]?"

"Yes, that is how He could talk to you in your heart, reveal Himself in nature, and then also say things in keeping with His word, ALL at the same time! He is spirit. He is always everywhere. He always has been and He always will be. His written word says 'before the mountains were born, or You gave birth to the earth, even from everlasting to everlasting, You are God" (Psalm 90:2).

"I can't think that big, Mother," Sammy confessed.

"I can't either, Sammy, but I can believe it because God said it," she replied.

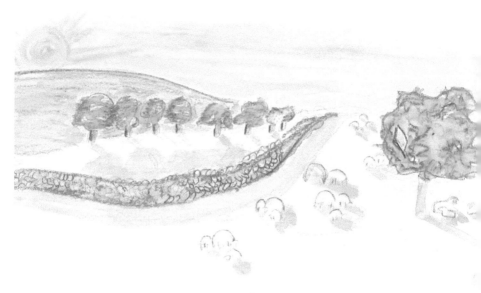

"And He never lies," Mother and Grammy said in unison! They looked at each other and laughed and bleated joyfully. Cammy and Sammy were amazed. "Did they just say that together?" Sammy asked Cammy. The boys nodded together, and they laughed too.

1. SPIRIT (AS IT REFERS TO GOD): *infinite, eternal, unchangeable in his being, wisdom, power, holiness, justice, goodness, and truth.*

1. SPIRIT (AS IT REFERS TO MAN) : *the immortal and immaterial part of man's nature that the Lord forms within him.*

CHAPTER 5

THE BIBLE

All across the wide field Cammy listened to the bleating of ewes to their lambs. Each lamb knew the voice of it's mother. Nobody else sounded exactly like Mother. Cammy could not only hear Mother with his ears, but also knew her voice in his heart.

As the day turned to dusk and the shadows grew longer, Shepherd knew it was time to take the flock back home to the barn. So many young lambs had joined the flock now, and He knew He had to be diligent to protect what was His. Many predators lurked in the shadows at the edges of the pasture.

"Here! Here to me, sheep! Here!" called Shepherd as He stood at the gated wall.

Mother's head lifted quickly.

Grammy's head lifted quickly.

"What is it, Mother?" asked Cammy as he lifted his head quickly.

"What is it, Mother?" asked Cammy as he lifted his head quickly.

"It's the voice of Shepherd, Cammy. Let's go!" And before she said another word, she was on the run! Cammy and Sammy were startled with this sudden move.

"It's time to go back to the barn," said Grammy as she firmly nudged the questioning lambs. The little family was altogether now. All the mothers were calling out to their babies. All the babies were calling out to their mothers. All the sheep were bleating before their Shepherd.

"How did you know that was Shepherd calling, Mother?" Sammy inquired loudly, but before an answer could be muttered, the clamoring[1] flock narrowed and quickly scurried through the gate, one at a time. The sound was deafening, but comforting all at the same time. They were all on the move to follow Shepherd.

Cammy called out louder, "how did you know that was Shepherd!?"

"Keep moving, little ones! Don't worry. Just follow!" Grammy encouraged.

It wasn't long before the barn was in view. The big door was rolled open awaiting the return of the flock. The scent of fresh hay welcomed them.

After a long drink from the fresh water bucket in their pens, mother spoke to the boys. "Cammy, Sammy?"

"Yes, Mother?" they bleated.

"Boys, close your eyes."

They did.

Mother bleated gently several times in a row and then asked, "Was that my voice or Grammy's?" The boys answered back "Yours!"

Again, Mother had the boys close their eyes. She whispered and winked to another ewe across the aisle², who then bleated several times gently.

"Was that my voice or Grammy's?"

The boys were confused. It didn't sound like Mother's OR Grammy's voice!

"You may open your eyes now," she said smiling.

"That didn't sound like you," Cammy piped up.

"That's how I know the voice of my Shepherd. I just know. When He speaks His voice is felt in my heart. When I follow Him, He brings me life. He is always in agreement with His written word too, so I can trust Him."

"Do you remember what God's written word is called?" Grammy asked.

"The word of God is called the Bible," Sammy answered proudly.

"Right!" said Mother.

Cammy had a very inquisitive mind so he asked, "how do you know God said those words that are written in the bible?"

Mother lied down and Cammy and Sammy
snuggled in with her. Grammy rested her chin
on the rung between the pens again. Mother and
Grammy liked teaching together.

*"Only the Spirit of God can make us willing to
agree to the truth, Cammy. But the Bible does
prove itself to be God's word because it bears the
characteristics of God. It sounds like Him."*

1Corinthians 2:13-14

"Just like Mother's voice will always sound like
Mother, and not me..." Grammy added, "and
certainly not a neighbor."
Mother went on. "Yes! And God's word always
agrees with itself from beginning to end, too! It
teaches and it encourages us. History proves God
over and over again. It all points to one person,
The Good Shepherd. It is all His Story." She smiled
because this gave her comfort too, not just her
lambs.

Grammy added, "The bible says it is all spoken by God, and is perfect for teaching, for reproof, for correction, and for training in righteousness, that the man of God may be ready for every good work" (2Timothy 3:16).

"What does 'righteousness³' mean, Grammy?" Cammy had to ask.

"It is a big word that simply means 'right living.' God's words tell us how to live right. And God's words always point us in the right direction and ultimately bring us life and peace."

At this point, Sammy was already asleep.

"It's been a great day in The Place of the Big Blue Sky, Mother," said Cammy as he yawned and laid his head on Sammy.

"Good night, little one. I love you." She kissed his head.

"I love you, too, Mother. G'night." Cammy let out one more big yawn and drifted off to sleep.

Tomorrow would always bring more to enjoy, more to teach, more to learn under The Place of the Big Blue Sky.

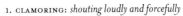

1. CLAMORING: *shouting loudly and forcefully*
2. AISLE: *a straight passage between rows or groupings*
3. RIGHTEOUSNESS: *the quality of being morally right*

Printed in the USA
CPSIA information can be obtained
at www.ICGtesting.com
LVHW072255201023
761655LV00017B/536